streetcake experimental writing prize
winners' anthology
2019

STREET CAKE
experimental writing prize

First published in 2019 by streetcake magazine,

124 Cadogan Terrace, London E9 5HP

First Printing, 2019

ISBN 978-1-5272-4426-9

Lightning Source
Chapter House, Pitfield, Kiln Farm, Milton Keynes MK11
3LW

Acknowledgements

The editors wish to thank the judges for their passion and
support.
Many thanks also to anyone who has helped promote the
prize.

Supported using public funding by
**ARTS COUNCIL
ENGLAND**

LOTTERY FUNDED

contents

foreword

This is the first year of our experimental writing prize but as editors of streetcake, we have been striving to support, publicise and champion writers for over ten years. We're really proud therefore to be honouring some exciting new writers in this anthology and see how they develop. The greatest part of this process has been talking to so many amazing writers and people who have a real passion for embracing the experimental style.

We also want to thank however, not only the winners, but every single writer who sent in their work and gave us the opportunity to consider it. As we read, we were gratified to see that we were correct in thinking there was a space for this prize. And in the words of our judge, Nik Perring, we all feel it's, 'a real joy seeing that the future of writing is in such safe, and talented, hands.'

We still think there's more work to be done too – more boundaries to push, more experiments to try, more surprising and unconventional twists to come. In the meantime, we hope every writer in this anthology is proud of their achievement because the hardest thing to do is send your creations out into the world. We hope this prize can honour their bravery and urge them forward in their writing careers.

We also want to thank ACE for funding this project and our incredibly supportive judges: Nik Perring, Sascha Akhtar, Ed Cottrell and SJ Fowler, who have helped us through this new project and any bumps along the road. Some personal thanks also to: Joe Ruddock, Simon Cusack, Alec Newman,

Paul Hawkins, Sam Ruddock, Whitechapel Idea Store, Laura Kenwright and Spread the Word, and everyone else who has shared and promoted our prize.

Please enjoy the read!

Nikki and Trini

Editors, streetcake

Consider an Apartment in Washington

There are only three things that matter in this life: chips, money and bubble baths. June's got a new girlfriend, Emse, who looks like a slapped fish. And June wants me to visit, because they want to have a baby, because the baby conversation's still on the table, because June thinks a baby will make Esme fall in love with her. The last time I heard a baby cry, there was blood and wine on the floor, and on my boots, and the house was never the same after that.

I'm living in Washington now, which is different from living in Blackpool, and no one here knows where Blackpool is on a map. They just peg me as a Londoner from the accent and the strong reek of gin. I haven't had good chips since I left Brighton.

Apartment #401. I don't know many people here. I know the Robinsons and their five-year-old Tasmanian devil, who screams like God is after him, who stomps around all night and punches his mum with big, meaty fists.

I know Mr. Addcock, a bloated giant of a man, and his pet parrot, who he's taught to say, "Look at the ass on that bitch!"

And I know old Ms. Creamer who says that there's a demon hiding in the vents of my apartment, that watches me while I sleep and wants to piss in my mouth. She's got thick hair all over her hands.

I know the weedy teenager who lives down the hall, kind of anorexic looking, who is selling drugs. Or exchanging drugs for sex with older men. I know that I'm softer than I used to be, that my hands still shake, and I can't take a beating like I used to.

And I knew Gina, bloodshot eyes and with three mouths to feed, who moved back in with her ex-boyfriend. He cracked her skull open with a baseball bat a few months later. A shotgun would have been kinder. The only things that matter in life are money and bubble baths, Gina said. Used to say.

I knew Cooper, too, the dimple-faced teenager who fixed my sink, who was fag-dragged in Kentucky and died three days later in hospital. Sometimes someone you care about holds your head underwater until your nostrils burn and you feel like your head is exploding. And Billie Holiday is playing on the radio, and it's a hot summer.

Well, June's got this new man and I'll always have Reo. He's an intellectual. "Barthelme! You must have heard of Barthelme!" He cocks his head to one side, like a confused spaniel. We're sitting on the living room couch in our big pajamas. On the table there are textbooks, a bowl of fruit, a revolver. He's strumming at his banjo and it's missing a chord. He puts too much faith in those books, in that banjo. He'll busk in New York until someone throws a Starbucks cup at his head and we'll see if Barthelme is there for you then. So much for saving humanity. Chips, however, might still have a chance. God I love chips.

Mr. Addcock is screaming and so is his parrot. I'm trying not to leave boot stains on the carpet. Don't shit where you eat. I wonder what parrot tastes like? Mr. Addcock's face goes bright red and he sleeps after I leave. Reo's banjo is missing another chord. I'm thinking about running my hands over that banjo and through his hair and about putting my tongue down his throat and in other places. Mr Addcock's tongue was down his throat, a policeman says, when they found him dead. I hope the bird gets the chopping block.

We take a bubble bath and we're too gangly for the tub. So I sit in Reo's lap with my legs either side of him. I can tip his head back and rake my fingers through his hair. His eyes are half-lidded and I kiss him and everything is warm and perfect. A part of Europe escaped the Black Death because they were Jewish and bathed. Water has a habit of pulling off everything red and black and washing away your sins into a sewer where they belong.

Reo touches the scars on my body: gunshot wound, stab wound, unfortunate encounter with a bagel. He says not all touch has to hurt you know. Only my touch does now.

I try to make him eat the bubbles but he tackles me and the bath water goes sloshing all over the bathroom floor and we flood the bathroom so badly it leaks through to the floor below us. Some old Russian lady comes round and screams at us and I explain there is a demon in our vent and that I'm going to fuck my boyfriend now.

There's an easy job, slipping a knife between a ribcage, and carving. Some old man wants it served to his grandson. I get done with that around midnight. I call June on the way home. The baby's here, I'm calling it Browny with a Y. Don't bother. I crawl into bed with Reo. His hair is mussed and he's drooling on the pillow. I pull his arms around me like a blanket and tremble.

Open up, police. There are men in jackets and they drag us out of bed by our hair. Get on your knees, bitch. They take the revolver from the table and point a gun at me and then Reo and then me again.

Murder is a strong word. Just like chips.

second place
L.H.S.

dematerialismin

I don't want to work on my own i don't want to its too much
pressure to just stare at myself in the mirror and try and push
ideas out like shits
What do they care nothing will come of me and my corpse
███████████ made me quit smoking it said in the terms and
conditions you better stop or ur card wont work anymore
I hate drugs only paracetamol for when my insides want a
chance to go outside
I take them on regular walks down the ███ Cross
I haven't found jesus yet only instant coffee in the chaplaincy
and a free lunch that you forget to go to
Last time the rice was pretty mushy, but then again rice is
pretty hard to get right so i don't blame them
I put my work into a big room and laid it all out bare, didn't
come to much, only made me realise how boring it is the
work that is
I eat a lot of fig rolls in the process and was shiting like a
mad man

God what a mess, did i mention i haven't found him yet?

I hate how self involved i am.
██
████████████████████

I actually have far too many things, more than i can carry in
one trip
It's actually a nightmare really difficult being a material

process person.

I think i'm going to head to the Internet and what not the computer room and have it all on there the physical world is far too ██

And i can't really use plastic cups anymore ██████ all the uproar.

The studios are empty, fleeting bodies come in for 50 minute appointments and scuttle off. Its like someones pressed pause and removed all the bodies and left only the desks. They look like classrooms when the fire drill goes

It's kind of hard i guess to know what to do when you could be doing anything, but also very easy so i'm not complaining

I keeping thinking back to cookie and the sex worker she was with. They thought i was also a sex worker
"been working then?"
"Yeah i guess" i reply thinking about the half hearted ██████
reading id done at my grandmas house the day before
"Where are you going?"
██████████
"Oh i know ████████

Apparently so do i
I'm shaken cookie and the sex worker talk about work, they don't really want to do it, they discuss but its good money
And here i am sitting here complaining about ideas
I'm starting to think that something needs to be done here

██

██████████████████

She keeps telling me to buy toilet roll before brexit
She's got 5 litres of olive oil and endless bags of rice and cans of beans in my old bedroom It seems as though i've been replaced with long shelf life food

Spent a tenner on floradix because im convinced im low in iron It tastes like shit
The mirror i put up keeps falling down

The books i borrow i never read, they just sit in my room for a couple weeks Until i decide they should go back home

I have a coffee flask, but i keep forgetting to bring it around with me
Last time i had one a long string on onion came with it, as vegetable soup had been in there before

Doing a shit always makes you feel better
Piss always makes you feel a little bit better

My face is kind of dry
The radiator is too hot

Galleries are often disappointing
I need to get a job
I got over my annoyance at whistling
Apparently if you straightened out the ████████ and pointed it straight to the sky it would as tall as the shard
It's very hard to explain what you do every day

I want to change my name to something else like biscuit cake Or charlie smith or Veronica corrupt
Ker█pt

Do you ever wonder if your grandmother hates you? Or if the stain on the floor is from a raisin
Do you like raisins? A Lot of people dont
Some people are allergic to nuts
The tube is pretty rough kind of loverble tho

Denise made me get my shit together
But im still a bit embarrassed because it's not quite all together Its intimidating being around people here

There seems to be a disconnect between email and reality

The work iv made this year is pretty meh

Im still scared of the ██████████████ i keep wanting to think of an idea to do there and do it to prove to myself that im not scared but i cant think of anything yet

I pulled the emergency alarm twice this year on the tube
One for a little boy who had a fit and once for a suited man who collapsed i didn't see him collapse, only his suited legs with shiney black shoes on sticking out like in the wizard of oz

The section of the tube between ████████ and ███████ is the loudest in the whole undergroud
I refuse to put my fingers up to my ears, the screaching scapres my brain, like a difficult itch to reach
I saw ricky gervais in a pub from a car
And ayyonline in ████████████
And djjdsport in a pub in ████
And that guy from qi in the library
Any Graham Norton in ████████████
And sam smith at a bar
And my house mates childhood friend really pinged in shefeild
And a fight in a big sainsburiys
And an uncomfortable silence on the 2█
And a loud American coming home from ████████ on a packe night bus

Im not a sex adict or a nicotine adict or perticually interesting when im drunk, i dont really enjoy having baths that much, more a shower person

But my face is quite dry

ill never forget the shock on his face

quickly scuttled

I wonder if i will ever make anything good I wonder if ill ever start smoking again

Maybe when i leave

third place
grace tompkins

Her

In the park I go to smoke there is a little brick shed with a wooden door. It is about as high as my waist and as wide as I am tall. Each brick is its own person and they swap over whilst I am sitting on it to see if I'll notice. I never do. Years of teenagers, rebelling with their own names in their hands and a comfortable bed in their parent's homes, have carved themselves into its body, with keys and pen knives and cans of cheap cider. Some brave souls have tried to carve into the bricks but they crumble too easily. The biggest letters on the door, the only ones I can read, are C and R. I hope whoever they belong to is happy.

From the roof of the shed, which dips in the middle so there is always a puddle, even in a drought, I can watch the people of the park. The under 12s training for their next match, the dog walkers pretending they are in control of their fleeing pets, the pigeons in the sky which is always a shade of grey.

I met her on top of this shed. She asked me if I knew her sister. I said I did not. I hoped it was the truth because she had the kind of face I only wanted to tell the truth to. Her voice was lilac wine, it caught in my ears like breathing in someone else's smoke and made me unsteady.

She sat next to me. I on the left she on the right, the puddle in the middle keeping us apart.

How strange we must have looked, like birds on a washing line.

I tried very hard, that first day, to tell her she was pretty but she wouldn't let me. She said she hated pigeons the way she hated the park, but pigeons were pretty when it rained and the park was pretty when the pigeons flew. I told her there were always pigeons flying. She pointed to one sat in front of us on the grass and laughed.

When she left that first day, she folded some words into a daisy and left it floating in the puddle next to me. It was at the bottom, brown, with my cigarette butts the next day when I returned.

Sitting on that shed she would tell me things, and I would tell her things and we would watch the people of the park and the bricks underneath us would change places and we would not notice. On top of that shed nothing in the world was invisible to us and we were honest.

One day she told me about her sister, who was a yoga instructor, and the argument they had had over who got to keep her father's second-best pair of shoes. I told her about my dad's tumour and the time I spilled hot chocolate over a very expensive suit.

One day she told me about her first love and the hairs on my arms would not lie down. I wished that I could be in love and the fact that she had been made me feel closed up inside.

One day she offered me whiskey and I said that for me drinking was like dreaming with less colours. I hoped it was the truth and I think it was because I can't remember her reply, but she still brought the bottle with her. So, one day I told her about fear. How it tasted when it bubbled up in my throat on Sunday mornings as I lay in a pool of my own sweat, having lifted out of a dream where I had broken my promise to myself.

It touched my lips and everything caught fire and the colours were so real and the joy I felt as everything burned was so real. I watched my mother's hair burn, I watch her scream and the fire overwhelm, with a smile on my face and a steady heart-beat. I tasted the liquor, and flesh melted away from bone. I did not care. I would have helped the fire burn, if it meant I could taste that feeling forever.

I was happiest in those dreams.

That was fear.

I thought she would run from my anger but she didn't. She put down the bottle and smiled my favourite smile. The sky was still grey and I could hear birds calling their evening songs. I was sure our hearts were beating in time.

The wind blew through her hair, intertwining my smoke with her body. My fingers in her hair. Her lips on mine, in a way that told me there was more to come if I was patient. I promised myself I would be patient.

I was always early and she was always late. We would talk and laugh and watch the world, the clouds pushed by the wind, the birds hopping and flying, children running, leaves falling from their trees.

We watched all of this because we could. Because it gave us a reason to be close, to feel each-others heat. Sometimes we watched the rugby matches, pretending we knew players on the teams, taking bets over who would be the first to get a bloody nose. I was better at this game than she was.

Sometimes we raced from the line of trees to our shed and laughed as our heads spun.

We spent time memorising each other, tentatively with words and lips or fingertips and stuttering breaths. We smiled a lot.

She had a chip in her front tooth.

She had a birthmark that spread across her right shoulder. I watched it until it spread over my mind and stayed there. I saw it, in puddles and trees and the static that ran through my closed eyes.

One day it rained so hard I couldn't light my cigarette. The puddle between us grew until it touched our thighs and flowed over the lip of the shed to the ground. She stood in front of me, I brushed wet hair from her face.

She told me about her sister, who was a yoga instructor and how they were still arguing over who got her father's second-best pair of shoes. She told me she hated him for doing this to them.

I wanted to tell her something that would help, but I didn't have anything good enough so I listened to the falling of the rain and the low mummer of recounted arguments. I reminded her she was not alone with my fingertips.

We held each other until the rain stopped.

The birds sang their evening songs but we did not go home. Instead we watched the sun melt into the tree tops and talked about flying away with the pigeons or burning this place to the ground, there wasn't much difference between the two in our minds. We carved into the wooden door next to each other, below C and R.

I had never seen her handwriting before.

We rested our backs against our names and watched the clouds clear and the stars come out.

We slept skin to skin. Soaking wet, in each other's arms.

She woke me with a kiss and told me to meet her later.

I tried. But the rain had taken hold of my body and kept me inside. Away from her. I called to apologise but she did not call me back.

Sometimes her tears woke me from dreams where I was trying to find something but couldn't. I was searching and searching but it was no use. I knew it was no use. The rain that splashed off my body was hers as I felt her lips on the back of my neck. I brushed the wet hair from her face and she brushed off my hand. I could not speak and she didn't. She just stared at me and the scar under her left eye flickered, as tears ran over it.

And then I was awake, alone in my bed with her tears running down my face.

One day I decided to walk until I wasn't thinking about her anymore.

At three in the morning the only people who are awake are not really awake. All the people who are strictly themselves are dreaming so we are not ourselves, we are the product of whatever it is we are taking or not taking. They are dreaming, and we are awake and wondering.

She was walking, towards the park. So was I.

We were not walking together.

Her skin didn't look real under the streetlights. It looked the wrong kind of soft but I still wanted to touch it. Someone walked next to her but I did not notice.

I smoked, sitting on the church yard wall staring at the cross which hung under the clock. The clouds were weighing heavy on the sky so the smoke rose and stopped to become cloud.

I was beginning to sweat.

The gravel of the path crunched under my feet as I made my way into the park. I had not heard their footsteps and I wondered now if the sky had muffled them from me.

They sat in our place.

A twig cracked under my foot and they looked at me.

Their eyes had the same kind of quiet smile.

It isn't something you can learn, that smile, it's something you are or are not.

They sat. She on the left, the shoes in the middle, her sister on the right looking at me. Tying and untying the brown shoelaces that sat between them.

She slid from the roof and took my hand. I tried to apologise but she wouldn't let me.

She took the unlit cigarette out of my mouth and replaced it with her lips, her teeth.

Her fingers intertwined with mine. Her voice in my ears.

There was no gap between our bodies for the rain to run through. Our lips smiled into each other. For a moment I couldn't feel the night or the clouds or the sweat finding a path down my back.

She was everywhere.

She was everywhere. Then she broke away.

In her lilac voice, she told me about her father.

He used to wear rings on his right hand. She never saw him without them. The scar under her right eye came from his wedding ring. The one on her sister's neck from a signet ring he had won in a bet. The one that cracked her rib, the one that pushed her down the stairs, the one that broke her sisters jaw the one that left her eye bloody and blue.

The man was a monster. He was a pair of shoes left to his daughters to keep them apart. He was the anguish in her eyes as she pretended not to care. He had taught these women how to inflict pain on each other. He had taught these women pain. He was nothing.

I listened, trying not to feel.

'He wanted to be buried with our mother, so we had him cremated'. Her sisters voice from the shadows. It mixed with the early morning birds so it was less words than music, but I understood.

For a while we, all three, sat on the shed, our bodies touching.

The sun slowly found the field in front of us, shifting until it lit our toes and knees. We talked about their father and my father, both of whom had died of cancer. We talked about the places we wanted to see, the people we loved, hated, knew, didn't know. I blew my smoke out towards the sun and used his shoes as an ashtray. They were soft leather, worn and repaired.

We talked about the park.

It was easy to sit with these women and forget there was anything beyond the hedges and rooves that surrounded us. Easy to forget that the sky wasn't something only we could see.

As the sun touched our faces her sister had to leave. I thanked her and she thanked me. Her blue eyes were hard on my face. She told me to leave his shoes for someone who needed them. Or for the rain.

Then we were alone in the park on our shed. With the morning sun and the birds singing their morning songs and the sound of cars starting and driving away. Her lips brushed the blue lines of my wrists again and again until they were the wind that moved the grass around us.

The first people of the park appeared. Early risers beginning their days before we had finished our night. They stared at us and we did not notice. We stared at each other.

And over and over we whispered. Care about me.

With our bodies. Care about me.

Again, and again. With our bodies. Care about me.

Please.

Care about me.

first place
leia butler

Word Ladder

Down

town and

torn but

turn,

burn. Re

born. Now

rise,

ride the

tide.

Time? Its

mine to

mind.

~~Go down the~~

~~word ladder,~~

~~Squared and~~

~~ensnared.~~

Fall

fail and

wail. But

sail, find

soil. A new

soul now.

Rise, you're

ripe, its a

rite. A free

kite, day &

nite- End,
on a good

note.

poetry 18-21 years old

second place
vthyl

complicity_12.3.9.exe

and hush
us / the red liquorice drop one
clinging onto structures of indiscretion escaping judges and black faux
furs

clinging onto the narrated, supreme pantomime
you trained machinery, a piece of polished ambiguity
the erringly wronged
the anxiety
    declared irrational
  yet necessitates the sentient contingent

where form and answers disconnect
  on the behalf of the insolent

carved eyes protruding, protracting, purporting
how much of the state of pity?
the red herring

how to locate and dislocate?
comfort in discomfort because discomfort is pertinent and a confessant

in your silent grudges between your two jellyfishes of scleras / sclerites

becoming this static two-dimensional impending, imploding, blasted
carnivore
how would you last, given the racially inscribed form of escapism?

reassured to reprehend and apprehend again
        apprehend   reprehend

.

civet coffee and reminders of a syntactical purple milieu
Silanised ponderal indexes

'You have salty figs.'
The correct question answers.

poetry 18-21 years old

third place
laurence waters blundell

Look at Me

All night cackling insanity to a five four simmering jazz.

Half-closed eyes empower full thoughts and a soaked

mind clouds unwanted chains.

Each heave of intention long planned, fully weighed

but still; eyes.

Eyes finished with a search just begun.

She speaks from within

'If to fall is to lose then consider me lost.

But I have moved closer to a sweet brown earth

 and seen faces painted high upon the trees'.

first place
ula taylor-reilly

Vermis Sanctus

I wonder if it likes how I taste and smell. I know what it tastes like, like dust and iron. Sometimes I suck part of it out of my throat up into my mouth, just to play with for a bit. I have to make quite a vigorous regurgitating motion to get the first bit up, then when there's some in my mouth I just suck repeatedly and it comes up really easily. It's such a fine, delicate thread that I can easily hold at least a couple of metres in my mouth. I like to push it into the gaps in my teeth, or roll it into a bolus and stab my tongue into it. Or I shape it into a thick rope and wrap it round and around my tongue, hauling up more length with every twist; it doesn't have enough strength in its body to resist my suction. Then I go still, to let it slowly reel itself back down, like a strand of wool gently being pulled. Once, I had a mouthful of it on the train and opened my mouth to show it to a businessman across the carriage. He probably didn't know what it was. I've been used to feeling it lurking near my oesophagus ever since I can remember, but when I was playing with it one time, I had too many overlapping strands sliding over each other in my throat at once, and I panicked, and just started chewing! Its body gave no resistance, and it was mild in flavour. I swallowed some, snorted some painfully through my nose and spat out the rest of the chewed up worm onto the desk in front of me, a variety of bloodless lengths in a puddle of sputum. They didn't wriggle. The uneven end raced back down my throat, that's the quickest I've ever felt the worm move.

I am located in the upper right quadrant of the house, the hottest organic mass in the building. If I stare down at my body for long enough I can observe rivers of skin gently undulating as lengths of worm get comfortable under the surface. It's occupying the right side of my chest cavity now and filling up my left arm. I'm so used to its presence, but I am still afraid to think of it going to my eyeballs, inhabiting my heart. I wonder whether it avoids those crucial places on its route so as not to injure me. Or maybe it goes to all those bits all the time and I'm just unable to feel it. I wonder if it's touching my brain.

I cringe when I think about how it sees everything I eat! I am one of the most mindless consumers, who lands in the centre of every algorithm, falling prey to the promotional aisle, activating my Nectar Card right on schedule. I may eat discreetly behind my hand, or select the daintiest and most rarefied snacks, or loudly justify my consumption to others, referring to the current seasonal festival or having only had a very light lunch, but every morsel arrives just as noisily as the next when the worm receives it as endless homogenous pap. I should really start making an effort and make sure it gets three wholegrains a day, as well as five fruit and veg, rather than endless mixtures of saturated fat and refined flour.

The worm is my very close companion. Immune to my stomach acid, it is acquainted with my most minute inner detail. No little witch's mark could be kept secret from it, and it swims over every polyp in my bowel. I like to think it would chew away a threatening mass, but I know it doesn't really have the strength to. At least I can eat what I like and not gain weight - I would probably be enormous if I didn't have a worm.

The first time I realised the extent of its growth was when I had a bad cut. I could see into my thigh, beyond the skin and fat. At first I took it to be a disease of the bone, but then

I realised it was worm, tightly curled to form an impenetrable mass, squirming slightly at the daylight. I often think of reopening the wound, to torture the worm, or to torture myself by looking at it, or to heave it all out.

There can't be much space in my body left for it to fill up, but it keeps increasing in size. I fancy that it could be a descendant of the Lambton worm, one of the ancient wyrms of Britain, who had huge goggly eyes and could wrap itself seven times around the hill. An unwanted catch from the river, it was disposed of in a well, which it eventually outgrew, and surged out of to devastate the village. Those are the eyes I imagine, although I know it is sightless, when I feel it swirling up into my stomach, giving me heartburn, waiting to be fed, or pushing into new territories to make space for itself.

It's really my own fault that I have become a host to a permanent guest. If I had had better hygiene, maybe if I had made some sensible lifestyle choices, with a balanced diet and plenty of exercise, if I had taken responsibility for my own body, got off my backside and done something about it, it wouldn't have got out of control. I did buy tablets to get rid of it, but they must be out of date now, and tablets probably only work for infestations contained within the digestive system. I'll keep them in the cupboard for now.

A colourless, directionless thing, profiting at my loss. A limbless, basic organism steadily overwhelming me, me: homo sapiens. But I couldn't accuse it of violence. It doesn't bite and scratch but sustains itself in the most elegant way I can think of; absorbing nutrients through its skin. Having evolved to outsource its more undignified labour it hardly has to lift a finger in order to survive. Unlike me, the ape, crudely pulverising foodstuffs, the worm has a certain purity. It would never belch, would never be guilty of the expulsive indiscretions that so repel me from other people. It has no foolish, wanting mouth, in fact it is inscrutable.

Without a digestive channel dividing the body into bashful halves it is intact. Without holes it is a perfect whole. A simple strand it is the first line in the sand, the original numeral. It is immaculate.

When the worm first got inside me, I was playing in a rock pool on the small, stony beach. We fished with little nets, hoping for a creature in the water, which was murky with clouds of sand disturbed by our jostling hands and feet. We imagined a primordial fluke, a water horse, an elusive ocean thing lurking for us to discover. When we caught a tiny leech, we watched it twist and flip in the net, and then threw it back in with revulsion and disappointment. When I see a photo of myself now, I work out whether it was taken before or after the worm. if it's after, I compulsively trace its shape over her picture, the obscene length irreconcilable with the plump body. A miserable bisection. I often wonder why it burrowed into my foot and not one of the other children. It must have been able to tell that I wouldn't bother to fight it – that I would make a good and passive subject to it for years to come. Or maybe I was slower and fatter than the others. Or maybe they are all infested too. Somehow I doubt that though.

My eye bags are so dark now, I can see the worm aging me fast. Look how far I can pull my skin out, see? I couldn't do that a year ago. And my hair, it's getting thinner, any vividness I ever had has been sucked away, I feel I look flat and prematurely lined, and I'm becoming translucent. I'm tired all the time and foggy in my thoughts. I'm sure it's responsible for my constant heartburn, and I've definitely had this headache since it filled up forty percent, and a very dry mouth. I should really drink more fluids, I'm sure it must absorb a lot.

When I inevitably die, unable to support the worm anymore, or thanks to one of the other afflictions clearly headed my way, I would prefer to lie face down on the earth and let the gentle annelids have my remains, but I will be packaged, unable to object, placed on a lunch tray and passed between many irritated strangers' hands. A little metal slot will determine my size, the quantifications will be recorded on my file, and when the x-ray detects an abnormality in my corpse they will cut out the worm, lay it over a turquoise sheet in an efficient and regular pattern, then weigh and measure it. The one to make the abominable discovery would be the hygienic and rational explorer, undoubtedly of fine physique, and all assembled would shake their heads at me, in simultaneous disapproval: she really let this get out of hand. It would probably end up as clickbait: 'Mile-long parasite found on autopsy table! Morticians horrified!', 'Greedy woman full of worm!' They would think me so grateful to finally be rid of my affliction. But would the chambers that are used to containing it breathe a sigh of relief? They might sag without their stuffing. I wonder, would it find a new host? No one would take on a fully-grown worm, surely. I hope it will swim out of the incision and wrap itself seven times around their throats.

second place
lauren orange

Definitely New

Now that I'm seventeen, I feel like I have lived long enough that I can start to feel the size and shape and weight of a year. Two years feels heavier than one, three heavier than two. I can estimate how much life could fit inside a given period of time. The idea of being twenty no longer seems like some abstract, far away age at which I'll be unimaginably worldly and everything around me will be different. It feels like it'll be three years away. I'll probably still be living in Swansea and driving the car I just bought from my mum's friend's daughter. But I could change my mind about my major or something by then, so you see what I mean about what's possible in different amounts of time.

In books they talk about youth like it's exploding with newness and discovery. But they also say it's part of being young that you don't realise that at the time. They always seem so sad about that. I sort of know what they mean, because I'm starting to sense there are periods of my life that have come and gone – adolescence, childhood. It aches a little in the dull way it hurts when you've lost something you can't get back. I hope it's not too late, but these days I try to realise when something is new and notice what it feels like before I'm too old and have done everything. I don't think it's too late.

I tried to explain this to my best friend, Amelia, and she was polite and everything but I don't think she really understood.

She and I are always so encouraging of each other that it can be hard to know whether she really gets me or she's just being supportive. Which is nice, I think everyone needs someone like that in their lives. I could check again but I don't think she really gets it. Not experientially, anyway.

Tonight, Amelia was at the beach with her family for the weekend. My mum was drunk in the living room and my sister had borrowed my car to see her boyfriend, so I didn't really have anything to do. I thought I kind of wanted to have sex. I'd only ever had sex with my boyfriend but we broke up six months ago and my friends and I had all downloaded dating apps at school. I started to get pretty excited about this idea. I thought it was cool that I could think of doing something today that I couldn't conceive of doing yesterday and probably thought I would never do. I felt young in a nice way, like all of my life was stretched out in front of me and I didn't know what it would look like yet. I also felt lucky that I can do so many things and have all this freedom. Lots of people don't have the opportunities that I do because I live in the UK and speak English and all that, and my mum doesn't have heaps of money but we're not poor or anything. I also had the feeling I knew a secret wisdom no one else around me knew. It felt like I was cheating to know it while I was still young and I wondered how many other people felt like this too. Like they realised how lucky they were to have lived their lives while it was still happening.

Eventually, I matched with someone on Tinder who was my age and didn't have pictures up of himself posing shirtless or with an erection under his pants or anything like that. Honestly, seeing that kind of men on there almost turned me off the idea, but this guy looked nice and I was pretty set on this whole thing by now. I started putting make up on and dancing around my room a little while I messaged the guy back and forth. I felt excited, but I was careful not to reply straight away because people always say you look too eager if you do that.

The guy was two years ahead of me in the school Amelia's brother goes to, and now he was studying something to do with economics at university, which seemed a little boring to me. I thought about telling him I planned to study fine art and social policy, but I got a little nervous about saying something personal if he didn't ask. And he didn't tell me anything about how he felt about his degree, so I left it.

Pretty soon, I was arranging to go over to his house, which was only a thirty minute walk away. It's funny how quickly this happened, but I guess it was a Saturday night so it was obvious why we were both on there. There's also something about Saturday nights that make you do weird things, like what they say about a full moon. People at school say they don't believe in that stuff, but I always say that's stupid because how can you know that for sure when you're only in high school and you've never even gone overseas or anything. I probably want to go to university, but there's no way I would do it without travelling somewhere first. It's nice to be so sure about something.

The guy lived with his parents but they were away for the weekend. When I arrived, he was drinking beer from a bottle and he offered me one. Usually, I would say no, but for some reason I pretended I liked drinking alcohol and I took it. Sometimes Amelia and I take wine from the kitchen and drink it in my bedroom, and we laugh and stuff but after a while it makes us feel kind of sad. The bottle he gave me felt weird and large in my hands, like I was very aware it was in there and I didn't know how to hold it. I felt like an actor in a movie and the bottle was like a prop that I had to pretend was real, like when they give the actors apple juice instead of whiskey. I didn't tell him I don't really drink, I just kept laughing loudly at everything he said and responding with "yeah" over and over again with different kinds of inflections.

The thing he did next I found kind of weird, although I didn't realise at the time. We were sitting on the couch and my body was positioned to face him in a way I hoped was flirty. There was a lull in the conversation and he said, "So, I take it you don't have a boyfriend?". I laughed and looked away kind of coyly and said "no" in an airy voice that didn't sound like it came from me. Then he said "good" and leaned in and started to kiss me. This might sound smooth or something, but like I said, I found it weird. Actually, I found it kind of sexist, but I don't think I could articulate or defend this idea. When you say something is sexist, people my age always roll their eyes, and adults smile like they're thinking about how young you are, even women. If I was telling it to Amelia I'd say that whether or not I want to kiss someone isn't a matter to be negotiated among boys, and she'd know what I meant.

After a few minutes of kissing, the guy sat up and whispered, "Do you want to go up to my room?". I said "yeah" too quickly and loudly and my voice pierced the air and hung around in it for a moment while he grabbed his beer and headed towards the stairs. I took mine and followed a few steps behind. Walking behind him was my first opportunity to think by myself in a while and it took me longer than usual to work out who I was. It was like when you get home from holiday and your dog is a little suspicious before they realise it's just you. I decided I was having a good time, but I couldn't really think properly and my heart had been beating pretty fast this whole time. I kept going with him to his bedroom.

You might think it's odd that I was confident enough to do all this when it was the first time I'd done anything like it. But it's not really that I was confident, it's that I was acting like someone who is confident. When I have to give a speech at school, I step into this persona where I do and say things like someone who is good at public speaking. It feels like I'm floating above myself watching this competent person give a speech. When I told my sister about it she said, "that's just the same as actually being confident", which seemed profound at the time. But sometimes when older people say things you have to think about it in private before you realise you disagree. I know now that it's not the same at all, because I'm still so nervous I feel sick and I panic beforehand and think it was a shit speech afterwards. A truly confident person wouldn't do that. I started to tell this to my sister another time when we were talking about school, which was sort of related but it was still like I wedged my topic into the conversation because I wanted to bring it up. And then I got flustered and couldn't explain it properly. It was a good idea in my head, but then it disintegrated and fell through my fingers like sand. Later, I told it to Amelia and it came out just how it was in my head and she understood completely. Amelia is so great it makes it ok there's this weird invisible film between me and my sister. Sometimes I get sad about it, like I miss my sister even when I'm in the middle of talking to her, but other times I think I'm lucky to have even one person I can talk to so well. My mum agrees I'm lucky to have Amelia. She says, "Jess, a lot of people never have anyone like that their whole lives", and she shakes her head with this expression that would make you feel really sad if you saw it.

Me and this guy started kissing again when we got to his bedroom. We were lying on his bed and he took off my shirt. This part was nice and I felt pretty relaxed. Or I was acting like someone who was relaxed, I don't know. Then he took off my jeans and my underwear in one go and then he put it inside. As I said, I've had sex before, with my old boyfriend, but this hurt anyway. He wasn't kissing me anymore and he was just moving up and down really fast on top of me and holding down on my shoulders. I tried to move but he didn't notice. After a while, it started to hurt like it was rubbing too much and I think I was pretty tense. I closed my eyes and thought about how I wished I was still in my bedroom feeling bored. I didn't realise how nice that was. I pulled my hips in like I wanted him to stop or slow down or something but he didn't notice that either. I realised I wanted to go but I couldn't think of a way to do that other than what I was already doing. I just made by mind blank until he finished.

It was quiet for a bit and then he said something about not having a big enough bed for me to stay. I told him I was planning to leave anyway and he said, "but you can stay if you want". I knew what he was doing even at the time. Usually I only realise afterwards when someone is dismissive of me. I smiled a weird smile that made me feel gross inside and put my clothes on as quickly as I could without making it look like I was hurrying. He told me not to walk and gave me directions to the bus stop, and he said I could also get an Uber. I smiled even though his car was there and he didn't offer to drive me. I also didn't have Uber. He said I should text him if I needed anything and I smiled again and nodded and this time said thanks. That was the worst part.

I started walking home because I didn't want to spend money on a cab. I thought about what happened in the background of my mind while I looked out for restaurants or convenience stores that were still open. I saw a small Indian restaurant with a neon sign in the window that said 'OPEN'. When I went inside I saw that it was half an Indian buffet and half a pizza restaurant with a guy standing there mopping the floor. The buffet looked depressing or like it would make you sick, so I ordered two large samosas from a glass dish on the counter and asked for a cheese and garlic naan bread to take away. I started eating the samosas while I waited for the naan and I had finished it all by the time I was about fifty metres out of the restaurant. When I was done I thought about how the samosas were big and oily and calorie dense and I felt sick all of a sudden. I turned the next corner and knelt behind a bush and made myself throw up. The spices were strong and acidic and I coughed a lot and my nose ran. I wasn't crying but my eyes were watering, too. I kept walking in the direction of my house, drinking the water I had in my bag and wiping my nose and eyes.

I thought it felt colder now than it did when I first left his house. I decided this was probably a bad experience, but it was definitely new so I wondered if I was learning something. I thought about some of the times I had been really alone, and decided this was probably the first time I had been lonely. Then I thought this was probably the kind of situation where you pay for a cab, so I stopped walking and faced the main road and waited for one to come past. I kept closing my eyes and then opening them suddenly and thinking "boom!", but it didn't make anything appear. I don't know how long I waited, but eventually a cab showed up. It always happens after you give up the game. The driver seemed nice but I just smiled and looked out the window because I didn't really feel like talking.

fiction 22-26 years old

third place
ana dukakis

YOU + the DARK + the DOOR

[LOOK AT   CALL TO   THINK ABOUT   , USE]

The Room

You wake up in **The Room**. It is dark. You have been in this DARKNESS for a while.

...

There are four WALLS and one DOOR. Otherwise, there is NOTHING, lots and lots of NOTHING.

...

You are alone.

...

> USE DOOR
You try the handle, but the DOOR does not open.

> LOOK AT DOOR
Hmm. There are scratches on this side.

> LOOK AT scratches
...But that isn't a valid object here.

> LOOK AT DOOR
The DOOR has a peephole, which is misty.
When you press your ear to the grain, you hear muffled voices.

> CALL TO

What do you call to?

> CALL TO DOOR
…But NOTHING happens.

> CALL TO WALLS
…But they stand, unmoved.

> CALL TO DARKNESS
…But NOTHING happens.

> CALL TO NOTHING
…And NOTHING happens.

…

> THINK ABOUT DARKNESS
Brrr. It has been here a while. At least as long as you.

> USE DARKNESS
You curl into a ball. Like deep-sea, the DARKNESS fills between your folded arms, your collapsed legs, your curled toes.
You wait for it to sink up and swallow you, but there is just more NOTHING.

> THINK ABOUT
What do you think about?

> THINK ABOUT anything, please, absolutely anything, anything outside this room
…But that isn't a valid action here.

> THINK ABOUT you
…But that isn't a valid object here.

> THINK ABOUT NOTHING
The NOTHING stands rickety in your head, along with other

thoughts. Soon, the other thoughts storm the NOTHING castle.

…

Why can't I break down the DOOR? Why can't I call through the WALLS?
It's cold in here. It's so empty.

> LOOK AT DOOR THINK ABOUT freedom CALL TO outside
…But that isn't a valid action here.

…

> LOOK AT NOTHING
…And NOTHING happens.

…

> THINK ABOUT NOTHING
The crumbled castle constructs once more. You have picked up these stones so many times before.

It is hard labour, and now you breathe, deeply. The breaths form a ragged shoreline around the castle.
They are your BREATHS.
…

> THINK ABOUT BREATHS
They are coarse but steady. They are a force that is deep-sea and buoyant. They are yours.
And since they are in this room, it must mean you are in this room.
You are still here.
YOU.

> LOOK AT YOU
Really, look at YOU: a shoreline.
YOU have gone so far, come so far, YOU really have.

And now YOU are in this room. **The Room** which has NOTHING and DARKNESS, and YOU, breathing.

The Room has NOTHING on YOU.
…
There is a way out, if YOU can only make it valid.

> YOU LOOK AT DOOR
YOU see the DOOR: the worn handle, the scarred wood, the misted peephole.
YOU hear the DOOR: the echoes of scratches made before, the muffled voices on the other side.
…
And there, finally: a key hole.

Which means there must be a KEY.

>YOU THINK ABOUT KEY
Which means the KEY must exist.
YOU feel a weight in your pocket.

> YOU USE KEY
Your BREATHS are shaky as YOU walk to the DOOR.

…

…

…

"Click"

…

> YOU OPEN THE DOOR

first place
michael sutton

kommunikation

if you were sensibly cooperative   not unreasonable
     we could do business   broken   tibia fibula radius
fractured skull   I leave you alone
     for a couple of minutes   and well if it was for erm
beneath the cloud   encrusted glow of
     moon that clings   that sighs   that pirouettes
sure of its own dormant essence   same as our Layla
     when she kicks me in the shin   but here we are
in this sacrosanct warehouse   when she steps on my toes
     as she slides off the monochrome rainbow
when we run out of red and yellow and pink and green
     orange and purple and blue   wake up
this is not a nursing home   if you were not intransigent
     to this stained glass sine wave
you would undoubtably succumb   spitting in a bin bag
     I was born underwater   in the lost city of England
I cannot be drowned   off the coast of Suffolk
     not meaningful enough for me   where goes the extra L
is it swallowed by the present like time   itself   probably
     not   if you were not so   what is in those eyes

ask the cat on the windowsill
     drenched in the bad spirit of things

pray for our sinners   now celery is the loudest food
     but you get nothing till you erm   a visit from G-d
all options on the table   yes the mystical economic
     sanctions   they float   like an aurora   in the night
and sting like an atom bomb   lord   make the nations see
     vermin vermin vermin   that men should brothers be
vermin vermin vermin   if you were not so   recondite
     we could make the news   the question   becomes
are you willing to   what is this   what new thing
     is this   doing   it must be doing   something new
and I commend this statement to the warehouse

second place
yvonne litschel

dogwalkslowly

I took a late dog for a walk
I took a dog with a slow walk
I took a dog with lukewarm water
                              don't tell people
        I'm trying to overtake you
        don't tell people I'm trying
                        to overtake you
                                    w conscious lukewarm water
                        I took a late dog
                                aside from anywhere
                        won't panic
        tell people who are trying to overtake
                                you won't panic
            I'm standing on my own
                            two feet late dog
            another everywhere I am
                            already calm take
                        dogwalkslowly down r

there she goes...

we have automatic air fresheners in o
the ugly ones hide behind family p
the beautiful ones sit beside the
mum doesn't change their b
they still breathe for me sn
undertones of x y and z
pump & hiss i can't
scents but this one
five seconds to
room   diss
settings wit
walks
wheeze
into

ur house
hotographs
m even though
atteries anymore
eeze for me release
  for me pump & hiss
name all of her favourite
    this one gives her forty-
drift   from lounge to dining
ipating as she goes   to adjust
h her nails before pump & hiss she
back to her   bedroom   one minute
s then squeezes back under the glass
 her frame
                              the one i like best

Lightning Source UK Ltd.
Milton Keynes UK
UKHW011253230819
348269UK00006B/181/P